<u>This Book is Dedicated to:</u>

My children- I'm sorry for every seizure you have witnessed me having, and all the fear you have of me having another. You are so smart and brave and beautiful. A mother Couldn't be prouder!

My parent's and my siblings, Sorry I was such a turd growing up, thank you for loving me and believing in me.

To my Partner -Present and Love of my life, Ben Daniel Heggie, thank you for all the above. I love you more than you know.

And finally, to the late Cameron Boyce, a brave and brilliant young man and talented actor, and fellow epileptic who was taken too early by SUDEP

(Sudden Unexplained Death in Epileptic People). To his family and his Legacy, The Cameron Boyce Foundation, which will be receiving a percentage of sales from this book. And where you can join the cause and donate at

<u>www.thecameronboycefoundation.org</u>

And all those who have or love someone who has Epilepsy or has died from SUDEP.

Yours in faith,

Elyse Yvonne Slater.

Copyright

Synopsis

She was treated like the plague; superstition denied her the privilege of friends.

The entire town, her parents included believed she was "The Devils Intended" ... that is to say, she was possessed and being kept for his return to this place! It was said the man she married would love her for all she was because that's the sort of women the devil was into.

When she came of age the town locked her in a cellar fearing Armageddon!

The Epileptic Girl

Elyse Slater

Contents

RELIGION

Growing up was hard. Learning was pointless, getting to school was impossible... Always sick, always sore, always something diabolically uncontrollable holding her back. What was the point of taking these medicines? It didn't feel like they worked very well. Infact they made her feel horrible! Sad, depressed, angry, paranoid, too tired, clouded, clumsy, stupid. Forgetful even confused.

When she was hit sometimes or got introuble, she was affraid and sad. She couldn't do anything right. She even started laughing uncontrollably, she didn't mean to. She wanted to cry... but ended up laughing instead, getting her into even more trouble. And had to change her medicine again after explaining what happened.

Her mother felt terrible having beaten her for it, but at the same time was at her whit's end. There were no hospitals, besides the St Claire Charity Hospital at the local church. Which was supervised by Sister Farrengarde, and even she felt hopeless to help the girl. And Farrengarde had no choice but to recommend her to the sanatorium held below ground. And managed by a presbytery of priests and pastors.

So, when Laura Serenna Carpena came of age, she consented to the townsfolk locking her in a cellar, but she feared that the worst was yet to come. She herself now believed she was possessed by an evil spirit. And felt helpless. She was forced to fast before exorcisms, she was basically starved and denied water or milk. This didn't help her situation any!

One day a white man, a rich outsider from America was inspecting the Asylums, for missions and discovered the girl, dirty and emaciated cowering in a corner below a window in her cell. He was a doctor!

“That girl is so beautiful, and yet, so sad! What is her condition?"

As he looked through her admission statement, he was appalled that beside her name all that it said was “Demonic Possession!”, That under care instructions the papers read; "to be ignored, except for being exorcised by the head priest. Feed and ignore. This one will not be freed.

The doctor enquired... “why ignored? … and exorcisms? You don't really believe she is possessed, do you?’

to which one of the Pastors replied...

“The Girl is possessed! She will try to talk and beg for help, but then she gets sick! She stops breathing, tightens! She shakes viciously...she chokes on drool, bubbling in her mouth, and blood comes out! We can’t move her when she tightens! She goes hard like wood, and we cannot help her when her mouth bleeds, if we do, she tries to bite off our fingers… she is *evil*! She is always possessed but we cannot exorcise her anymore, because the demons will not budge, instead they hurt her more. They don't respond to exorcism the way they are supposed to! Whatever possesses her is more powerful than any demon we know of! The Devil is keeping her! He *will* come for her! This… is the only safe place for her. And the only way to keep the devil from using her!

That night the girl became possessed over and over so, the doctor called for his helicopter, and he told the priests...

“I’m taking this girl with me! I can help her!”

The priests were objecting insistently.

“No!” they said... “No! It's you... you are the Devil! Gringo! You have come for her at last!”

The doctor replied,

"If I my intent was to have my way with her, wouldn't it have been foretold in the bible? Your faith is twisted by the fear of things beyond your understanding!"

“This *girl* is *not* possessed! I have seen more like her; she has Epilepsy!”

The priest responded stammering!

“Ep-epilepsy?” They asked.

“Yes! Epilepsy:" he said.

“I need to take her to a hospital, in the states! Please, if she stays here, she will die! I can save her life, but I must take her NOW!”

Urged the doctor.

The two priests looked at each other, “Okay, you take her but bring her back when she is well! For her mother's sake"

“I will be in touch, I promise!” The Doctor said, as he lifted her limp body onto the stretcher and into the helicopter which he radioed for earlier and took off into the night.

Two weeks later he brought the girl back to them for a visit. She had colour in her face and had put on some weight she spoke so elegantly, calmly, gracefully. She seemed a to be a smart sweet girl!

She said; “the doctor saved me, he helped me! I take tablets three times a day, and I haven’t been sick for over a week.”

The priests were impressed but they still didn’t trust these two together they suggested; “Okay, now that she is healthy, she can stay here with her family!”

But the Doctor refused; “No, we need to continue observation, and she needs to continue taking medicine. It is a particular type of medicine and there isn't any available here! You don't even have a proper apothecary. If she stops taking it or it wears off and she gets used to it she will become sick again!” He replied.

The priests sneered, they were offended by the man's words. They replied to him; “We have medicine here the local store has many herbs and formulas! You either fixed her or you didn’t! This girl is still enrolled in our care now that her demon is absent she can find god! God will save her! He will watch over her!”

The Girl became scared she did not want to stay with the priests but the brothers restrained her and locked the doctor in a cell! They called him a liar and said he was crazy.

“We will show you Devil! You may not have let us witness your lies but you are blessed to witness now our miracle! You will see Gringo, the TRUE power of God!”

Then they spoke directly to Laura; “We will take away your witchcraft medicine demon woman... So that the lord can TRULY heal you!”

With that the priest in charge tossed her pills in the trash and threw her in the cell opposite the doctor... Later that night the priests gathered around her. “The time has come!” They restrained her; they yelled at her, they babbled in tongues, they flicked holy water at her and pressed crucifixes hard against the four sides of her head, they grabbed her face and the top of her head and gripped her tight and shook her.

And then she started shaking without help, she started to tighten and flex she bit down hard and frothed at the mouth, but they kept at her.

The doctor was hysterical now; he was losing his shit! He had grown attached to her and he knew better! He knew now, this had become inhumane and vanity based! He was enraged because he could not help her from inside this cage.

He started to beg them; “please, please. I can save her please I brought an emergency kit for her let me save her please I can show you how please I can prove it's a medical condition!"

The priests stopped and stepped aside one of them let the doctor out of his cell and another brought him his bags... by now it had been ten minutes since she started convulsing!

The doctor quickly removed an ampule from his bag and opened it he tried to squeeze the contents under her tongue, but it was too late her jaws were tight shut.

He grabbed a vile the liquid inside seemingly similar but this time he extracted it with a syringe. Quickly, but carefully he injected the syringe into her shoulder. This caused her to bleed a little, but only because they couldn't hold her still. It took a few seconds, but her body started to relax and she seemed to be sleeping. As she started to approach consciousness her eyes rolled and her stomach convulsed. As she reached toward the doctor, she vomited, and vomited, and kept on vomiting. She started trebling and couldn't stop. Her stomach was too upset.

"Hold her away from her vomit so that she doesn't drown in it!"

Called the doctor as he reached for a new vile.

It was a different color and had a different name! The doctor thought to himself; "she won't be able to keep this down orally! I'm going to have to make an injection into her abdomen!"

He pulled out a fresh needle and extracted the drug, and then he stuck her in her abdomen with it. It hurt! And she moaned... she went to throw up but nothing happened, then again... but nothing came up. Her tummy kept contracting but gradually slowed to a halt. She was dead tired now.

"Get me her pills, now!"

Urged the doctor.

One of the priests brought the bin over and pulled out her container of pills. The doctor grabbed a bottle of water out of his bag.

“Just one!”

He exclaimed.

The priest handed a single pill to the doctor...

” Open your mouth Laura, take your medication!”

pleaded the doctor.

She dropped her mouth so the doctor could drop the pills in, then he put the bottle to her lips and tipped it carefully.

” Drink, drink! Good girl.”

The doctor sighed in relief.

Laura blacked out and slept for about forty-eight hours waking only for her meds and a couple of mouthfuls of yoghurt.

When she finally roused herself properly, she noticed that she was in a pretty flash room, in the most comfy bed she had ever slept in in her life... And the doctor was sitting in a rocking chair facing her. He hadn’t left her. But he was asleep!

As she called him he awoke and he said. “Laura I bought you a passport and a citizen ship... The priests signed custody to me. They have agreed your better off in my care they asked me to convey their apologies you don't ever have to see them again if you don't want to. You are free to start a new life here in America with me, if you like you're in charge of your own life now."

"Thankyou" she replied.

"Umm can I use your toilet?"

"Your toilet! Laura this is your home now too! Come I'll show you where it is" replied the doctor.

"Thanks.... Umm," she hesitated.

"Stanley... my name is Stanley" replied the doctor.

She closed the door and went to the toilet.

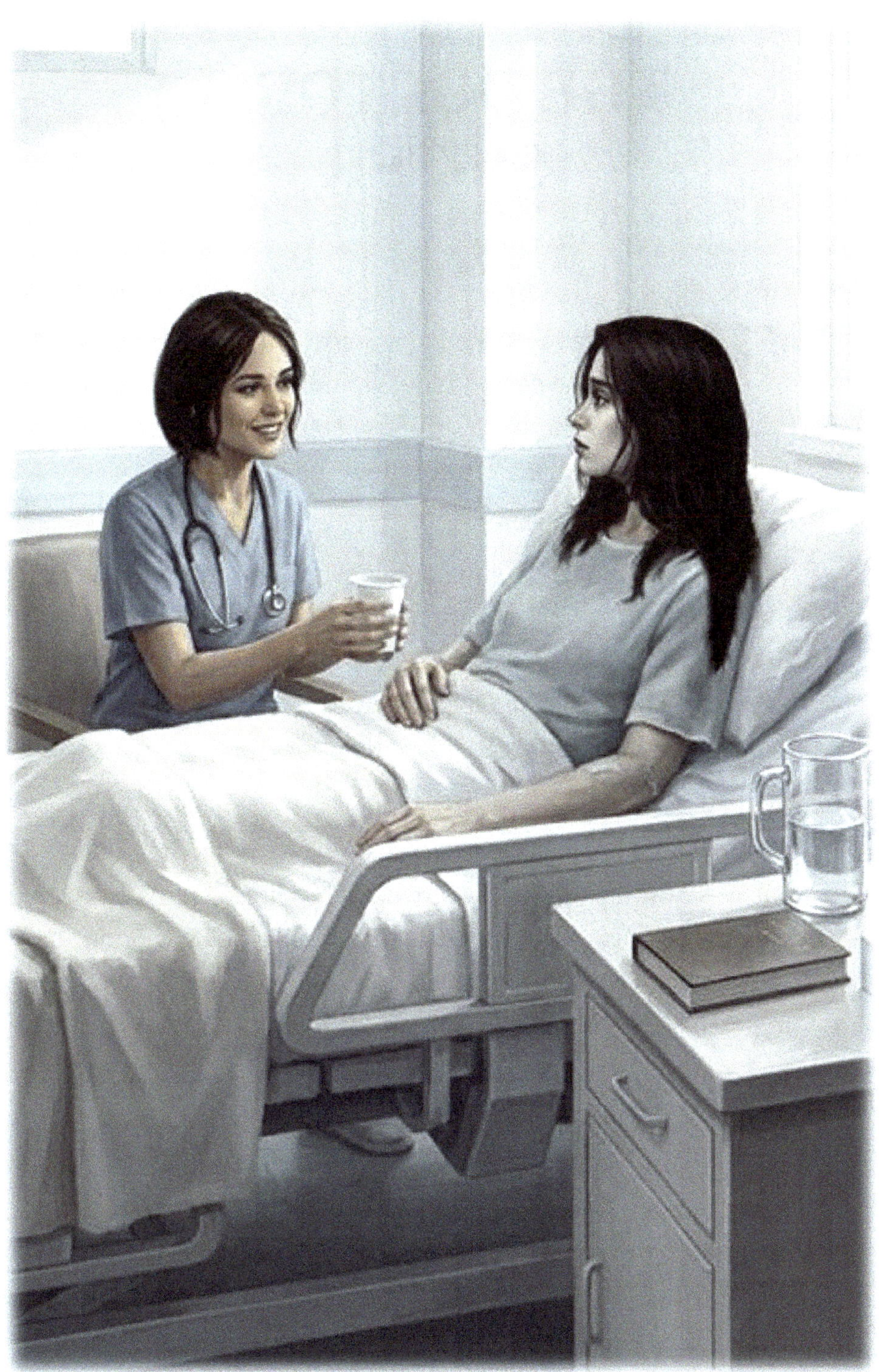

THE DOCTOR'S SISTER

The medication started to wear off after a few months just like the doctor said it would! Though her blood tests still showed a sufficient amount of Epilem, the seizures she was having clearly showed the dosage she was on was not good enough...

She was moved to the neurology wing in the nearest hospital for more tests and observation. They did many tests to discover the main causes and triggers to her typical seizures. During the E.E.G. her neurons reacted in a ghastly way to light they suggested bright lights or

repetitive flashing was definitely a trigger. So, Laura was given an eye patch to sleep with while in the hospital but was still disturbed and provoked by the sound of call buttons, yelling, chattering, squeaky shoes, and the snoring of the other patient... Laura became sick after an hour of trying to sleep through the petty ruckus.

The doctors decided to repeat the E.E.G. using sounds and it was confirmed noise was an irritating trigger. So she was given earplugs... Laura could still hear through the earplugs but what's more they were uncomfortable to sleep in.

Finally, the doctor decided to ask her what else was bothering her it seemed no matter what they tried she still fitted obviously disrupted sleep and being overtired and frustrated was a trigger... And the hospital was no place for an epileptic her high keen senses and high electro magnetic field made her a static target for disruption... She slept fine at home but no matter how comfortable they tried to make her at the hospital she seemed to suffer from sleep insomnia.

One of the doctors joked, “don't have kids then will you you’ll never get sleep!”

But Laura shrugged she thought the comment a bit inappropriate and very random. She was not considering this idea for the near future at all she was too young! “Maybe one day?” She thought “if I get better... why would I put myself through that or risk putting kids through me?”

“Do you have a boy friend?” Asked a meek voice seemingly amused... another nurse, although this one seemed a bit nicer than the others did.

“Ahah?" Exclaimed the doctor suspiciously as he approached Laura. It was Stanley!

“I see you two have already met! Laura, this is my sister Gabby she works here too!” He said smiling.

“Oh!” Exclaimed Laura curiously “I had no idea! Is that why she’s dressed like a nurse and taking my obs'?” She teased sarcastically.

"No!" Said gabby spitefully standing with her hands on her hips...

"We hadn't introduced ourselves yet, because you interrupted our conversation! But I suppose that's my fault isn't it I knew who she was, because you talk about her all the time Dr. Obsessed!" Gabby giggled... Thrilled with cleverness knowing she was going to get away with it...

Laura was blushing now!

"Stanley told me you'd be here today Laura, I had to meet you for myself... I can see now why he can't shut up about you! Look at you, you're gorgeous!"

Laura blushed deeper. "No Gabby, I don't have a boyfriend, I've never had a boyfriend I've never had any friends except for Doctor Stanley!" Replied Laura. "How's that? You're too pretty not to have any friends!" Asked Gabby befuddled. To which Laura replied, "Because they're afraid of me! The entire town thought I was possessed, because of my fits!" Laura sighed...

"Well, that's just stupid!" Gabby started to raise her voice outraged. "I mean that's just, just terrible! You mean you had NO friends at all growing up?" She asked.

"Nope, well... no human friends I had some rocks and snails and I caught a lizard once but that's it!" Replied Laura indifferently, puffing her cheeks and eyeing her restless thumbs and fidgeting with her catheter.

"Well, that just sucks!" Huffed Gabby.

"I've been a nurse on this ward for 15 years and I'm sick to death of being told by every kid who comes in here that they have little to no friends because they're treated like they have the plague!" Gabby was starting to pull out her hair!

"Maybe you should ask the Senator to fund a community education program that goes around educating classrooms about epilepsy, Gab!" Chuckled Stanley. Then he whispered to Laura, "He's Gabby's fiancé you know!" Stanley laughed again.

"It's not funny Stan! You know what? I will ask him! Wait and see! Things are going to change!" Gabby scorned him, then she smiled and whispered to Laura; "Ben over there in the next bed is only a little older than you! He has epilepsy too, why don't you talk to him when you get bored... he's very sweet." Gabby gave Laura a nudge, and as Laura looked up she saw Gabby shifting her eyebrows cheekily and Laura looked on, confused.

"Okay?" She replied "I would! Thanks, Gabby?" Laura replied.

As Gabby looked at Stan, she smiled pleased she had gotten a seemingly concerned, jealous reaction out of him. "Bye Laura, see you in a little while." Called Gabby as she left.

"Bye," muttered Laura exhaustedly as she peered over at the boy who was focused on his notepad. "Jeez she's a chatterbox Stan, I'm exhausted! Is it okay if I take a nap?" Asked Laura.

“Yes, my sweet! No tests are scheduled for two days! Sweet dreams Laura!" He said.

“Good night, Stanley!” She said quietly, smiling. Then Laura put on her eye patch and started to doze off!”

During the night Gabby monitored Laura she noted her heartbeat as it freaked out when Laura seemed to hold her breath in her sleep and took note of Laura's twitching and ticking as Gabby tried to check her blood pressure while she slept.

Laura started twitching again and startled Gabby as she was preparing Laura's new dosage, so she watched her carefully! Then she gently woke Laura to give her the new dosage, “Take this and go back to sleep deary!” She whispered.

Laura took her meds and did as she was asked and as Gabby looked on she noticed the twitching start to settle down and slow as her heartbeat became steady again and her blood pressure went back to normal.

“Thank goodness” sighed Gabby relieved and jotted down the improvement on her chart. “I hope it lasts longer than the last one!” And she sat back at her desk and sipped her tea slowly and relaxed now confident that if she dozed off everything would be fine and lucky for her it was!

THE BOY IN THE NEXT BED

The next day as Laura woke up her eyes scanned over Ben's bed...

"Gone? But where?" She thought. And as her eyes searched the room for the nurse, she spotted him walking back from the bathroom. He was still writing in his notepad and chewing his pencil. However, before he made his way to his bed, he went straight up to Gaby's desk, tore a few pages out of his book, and handed them to her. "Can you send these for me?" He asked.

"Just one envelope, Ben?" Gabby replied.

"Yes!" He said.

"I'm sorry I couldn't fit it all on one page," Ben said apologetically.

"That's Okay sweetie, I'm used to it." Gabby sighed.

"Thank you, Gabby!" Smiled Ben. And he continued on his way to his bed.

"Excuse me?" Said Laura.

"Huh, who are you?" Asked Ben curiously.

"Um...I'm Laura." Replied Laura.

“Oh? I’m Ben!” Proclaimed Ben.”

“I’ve seen you using that a lot, can you write? Or were you just drawing?” Asked Laura.

“No! I can write!” He insisted.

“Who were you writing to?” Asked Laura.

“Why do you want to know?” Ben replied curiously.

“Well, you write forever but you only gave the nurse three pages.” She explained.

“So what?” Ben shrugged.

“Well, I thought there would be more?” She finished.

“There was more, but sometimes I change my mind about what I want to say in my letters and have to start all over again!” Ben explained.

“But why do you have to start again?” Laura asked.

To which Ben replied...

... “Because I’m writing to my girlfriend, okay? And I want it to be perfect!” He burst, annoyed.

"Sometimes I feel like she'd want me to keep her updated, and other times I'm worried that I'd be putting a burden on her that's out of her control. And making our relationship all about me, and I don't want her to feel like I don't love her.

“Don’t you have a boyfriend?” He badgered.

“No!” She replied, "How come you do?” She asked.

"Well, I used the internet and put in who I was and who my ideal girlfriend would be and got some return matches, and one of the girls I talked to, had a brother who has epilepsy and he died, so she wasn't scared of catching epilepsy like the other girls in my neighborhood or school. Instead, she seemed to care about me and was at first worried I'd die like her brother, and then her mum told her that he got epilepsy from a bunch of tumors that grew rapidly in his brain. She wanted to move in with me and care for me and look after me she thinks I'm attractive and funny and more mature than the other guys my age... She said that I was almost as mature as she was but she is the same age as me!" Ben explained laughing and went on to say; "she's going to come and pick me up from the hospital tomorrow."

"But if she's picking you up tomorrow, why are you sending her a letter?" Asked Laura.

"Ha ha!" Laughed Ben.

"Gabby's not putting them in an actual envelope, she's scanning them onto the computer and attaching them to an email to my girlfriend titled from Ben! Gabby likes to help but I suppose she probably gets annoyed when I give her my letters because she has to set aside time to scan and send them. She has got her day filled!" He explained.

"Say?" He exclaimed wondering.

"Do you like any of the doctors? Like maybe, say, I don't know, ooh, Dr. Stanley?" This question was wry and coy.

"What?" Spat Laura blushing.

"Do you find Dr. Stanley attractive? Yes, or no?" He pried.

"Err..." Laura's face took an awkward expression

"*They're all in on this, I bet anything they're playing stupid... but where's it going?*" She thought to herself.

"Oh, that's okay!" Said Ben, chuffed with confidence he had his answer.

"I get it, you don't have to talk about it if you don't want to! I mean if you're afraid he'll hear you talking about him..." he started.

"That's not fair!" Snapped Laura "I'm not afraid of being embarrassed."

"Yeh, you're right!" Said Ben; "He probably already has a girlfriend. Right?"

"I don't know, maybe? But I've never seen one at the house!" She teased back.

Just then the doctor slid the curtain back, and Laura's face froze as she looked at Stanley and blushed and hid her face with her bed blanket.

"Ha ha ha, that's hysterical! Dr. Stanley, she is so funny!... Did you see her blush? Oh my god! She just said she lives with you and yet she has no idea whether or not..." But Ben was cut off before he could finish.

"That's enough teasing out of you for one day Benjamin!" Called Stanley; "Leave Lovely Laura alone or I'll tell your girlfriend." He teased.

Ben chuckled; "Lovely Laura..."

"The cafeteria is open now anyways; I'm going to get some grub!" Ben said.

"I guess I better go and get something to eat to then, huh?" Shied Laura.

"Not so fast missy! What was all that about, hmm? Never mind! How would you like to join me for lunch today Beautiful?" Asked her handsome doctor as he held out his hand.

Laura blushed deeper again and giggled girlishly and replied whilst biting her fingernail; "Okay."

"We can eat in my office if you don't want to run straight into Ben again." Offered Stanley. "Um, sure" said Laura flipping her curls to the side bashfully, semi-flirtatiously and smiled.

And off they went.

THE PROPOSAL

On the way to the cafeteria, Laura was sort of nervous. She stared at the floor and scanned around to see if anyone was watching, but they weren't. Gabby was keeping Ben's mouth occupied listening to him spill the gossip at the table they were sharing.

After Laura they had their food Laura and Stanley made their way to his office. Stanley held the door open for Laura and then closed it gently and locked it behind him. Then he drew the blinds and turned on the desk lamp so they could eat in peace.

They were halfway through their sandwiches when Stanley declared; "I do love you! You know?"

"What?" Laura replied in shock; "but I thought,". He stopped her.

"Laura, I fell in love with you, the first day I saw you, imprisoned in the cellar of that church, I want you to stay with me forever! Please, come back home with me after your E.E.G scan tomorrow?" Stanley pleaded.

"Okay, I will but why." Laura began but Stanley cut her off again.

"Be mine Laura? Please won't you say you'll be my bride?" The doctor was on his knees now, and Laura was by now as red as a ripe tomato she tried to hide her face with the last half of her sandwich which felt cool against her flush face, as Stanley swooped around beside her and swept her left hand off of her chair and fixed himself on one knee.

"Please Laura, please?" He begged and sighed; "don't you love me?"

She cradled his face immediately to stop him from thinking about it anymore.

"Of course, I do silly... and if you really mean it then, yes! A thousand times yes! Of course, I'll marry you!" And she gave him a kiss on the forehead.

Then he revealed the ring. it had three heart-shaped diamonds on it. The first was blue representing the past, the second was pink for love representing the present, and the third was white representing a promise for the future yet to be filled.

He slid the ring onto her finger and stroked and kissed her hand, and threaded his fingers through hers and led her arm to his waist, and held her in his embrace.

Then he kissed her forehead, then her nose and her eyes, and then her cheeks, below her ears, on her neck and her chin, the corner or her mouth... He lingered there for a moment, and then he dragged his smackers across her top lip. He kissed it slowly and gently then her bottom lip but this time he pulled on it a little and gently licked the underside of her lip.

To Laura this wasn't just nice and romantic it was cheeky and playful and an excruciating tease, her thighs felt tormented!

He wove his hands under her arms which were lifted a little the moment her arms broke free she ran her fingers through his hair tugging it involuntarily in torment.

Stanley grasped the tops of her shoulders and leaned her backward as he went for her collarbone kissing it, every inch of it! Breathing deeply as he trailed his nose along her neck and bit it gently and then back down to reveal her breast and sucked on its nipple.

It was go time! Neither one of them could wait to rip each other's clothes off. Laura specifically was hung up. She had to wrap her legs around him and crush him or she would explode!

He laid her down on the carpet, gently lifted her dress and spread her thighs to get closer... As he kissed her every rib and caressed her tit, he started going down, slowly dragging his tongue, kissing her down the center of her abdomen tonguing her navel, and French kissing her hips. He kissed her nickers dead center and breathed on them heavily as he hooked the waistband with his index fingers and slowly pulled them off.

He kissed her flesh and licked her vulva and sucked on her labia. He tongued her clitoris!

Laura's face spasmed in ecstasy, she wanted more, but she also wanted IT!

As he licked her vigorously her jaw dropped and her eyes clenched shut and her fists tightened around his hair... She couldn’t stand the anticipation anymore! She pulled his shirt off and sat up and went for his belt! So of course, he assisted.

He stood up and stripped off his slacks and boxers. He kicked off his shoes and yanked off his socks, the left and then the right. He got back down to the floor and positioned himself between her legs but couldn't see. So, Laura desperately grabbed his throbbing cock and guided him in!

She was so wet!

At first, it hurt but only at first, he wasn't trying to build her a chimney or anything so she straight away began to enjoy herself. As he continued he got harder and fatter and could it be... Longer? What ever it was it felt great and she wanted more. She could feel him rubbing against her walls! In and out, and in and out. More, more, more! She wanted to say but she was feeling shy. She wrapped her legs around him and held him tight digging her heels into his buttocks!

She held on to his shoulders and bit her lip as he began going faster and deeper. He pushed her along the floor supporting her neck! It wasn’t until they had nowhere to go but into a wall before they both came her just before he pulled out and then came all over her navel.

He seemed to shiver a bit as he emptied himself onto her, and kissed her. Then he rolled onto his back and hit his head on the leg of the phone table.

“Ooh!” He exclaimed and as Laura rolled over to see what happened, she giggled when she realized and so did he.

Stanley got up and gave her some tissues and helped clean her up. And before he put his clothes back on, he kissed her sparkling ring finger and helped her dress.

“You should finish eating. You don’t want to look shaken when you go back to your bed... Here!” He passed her a can of coke from his bar fridge.

“Drink this it’ll cool you down and wake you up a bit! I’d imagine you're a bit tired and thirsty after all that!” He explained.

“I’ll see you tomorrow for your test he continued as he walked her back to her bed. Then we can go home, together! And remember I love you!” He said and he kissed her on the lips in front of Gabby and Benjamin.

“I love you too!” She replied cradling the foreign object on her finger and hopping into bed.

When Gabby came back to take her blood pressure Laura asked if she could have a shower.

To which Gabby replied “Yes, but don’t wash your hair again or we won’t get a proper reading tomorrow!”

So she didn’t wash her hair. But she certainly slept well that night she’d exhausted herself thinking about what happened at lunch up until bedtime. Gabby noticed she had the biggest smile on her face during sleep. She also noticed some blanket clutching and Laura talking in her sleep. Could have only been imaginary things, but Stanley and Ben and Gabby were mentioned in her mumbling... just things like;

"Come on let's go!", and "Ner ner stupid Ben! Suck eggs!", "I love you too Stanley!", and "Jeeze, she's a chatterbox, that Gabby!"

Poor Gabby she felt offended for a second then thought; "maybe that was a bit of an overwhelming first impression... But it was just because I was excited I'm not always like that! I don't think. But then again maybe I am compared to her but I suppose how many people does she actually talk to?"

Then Gabby chuckled; "Oh well, she'll get used to it!"

A VISIT BACK HOME

One night back at the house after they had just made love in their luxurious bed, Laura turned into deep thought as Stanley was holding her. And Stanley noticed her concern. “What’s the matter beautiful? I wasn’t too rough was I?” He asked.

Laura blushed; “no, that’s not it at all!” She explained, “it’s just that for some reason I want to go back and see my mum. I want her to see me better, and I want her to be proud of me! And I’m starting to want to have the wedding there too! I want to invite the whole town and rub it into their miserable faces and get the church involved to prove I’m not evil! And also... I’m afraid Stanley.” She said worried.

“Of what dear?” He queried. To which she replied; “What if there are others there like me? What if there are no real doctors down there? What if there are others who are suffering the way I did? There aren’t any medical centres like there are here! The only prescribed medication the doctors give down there are cactus juice, alcohol, cod liver oil, crushed flowers and masturbation! They need to know how to diagnose treat and care for this disease and they need to develop a community support group like we have up here! If the are others, they are still suffering! And...” She was going to keep jibbering but Stanley managed to stop her.

"If there are more, then of course we must help but tonight lets focus on us Princess, please? Put it out of your mind until then, hmm? I expected as much when I first thought about us getting married, and I've already made arrangements! However it is odd you brought it up, because I was going to surprise you at dinner! We fly out tomorrow, but, heh, I suppose the surprise has just been ruined! Do you still want to go out for dinner, or shall I cancel and order Chinese?" He asked

Laura blushed again, ruined surprise or not this was still shocking, exciting, happy news the fact that Stanley had already thought of it and wanted to surprise her over dinner only made it all the better; "He's so romantic!" She thought.

"Um... Chinese!" She said. "The lights in the restaurant make me feel hot and dizzy and give me a real headache... the constant hum of rambling randomly rising voices doesn't help either they put me on edge. It was a nice thought though! Maybe next time we can find a quieter spot? She suggested.

Stanley chuckled. As if they were going to find a fully licensed well credited top restaurant in town with no people and poor light. Not like he cared...

"Of course Laura, Chinese it is!" He announced, with the following question; "what would you like?"

"Hmm, something different. But I can't make up my mind." She flicked through the book at least twenty times tracing each list repeatedly like she was colouring in.

“It all looks and sounds really good!” Laura explained staring at the takeaway menu like a piece of abstract art... She obviously wanted Chinese but was too distracted by what had just happed to focus on the takeaway menu. “I’ll tell you what Stanley, you decide!” She remarked impishly.

“What?” Asked Stanley. To which Laura replied; “oh, you know! I can’t decide I like them all... Surprise me!” She giggled now, Laura thought herself very clever as she headed for the sofa and snatched the remote. “I’m going to set a reminder for The Late Late Show With Craig Ferguson, he’s so funny!”

“Hmm!” Stanley growled; “I wish you’d go to bed earlier than that it can’t be good for you to stay up that late glued to the television! You’re not out of the woods Laura you could still have a seizure if you provoke yourself on medication!”

“Actually to tell the truth honey, I am dead tired by the time his show comes on, If he didn’t sing that cheeky bed time song at the beginning of the show I probably wouldn’t hang around to see the start then there’s the extra long lengthy applause and dicking around but the commercial breaks are a killer they’re boring and go forever I just want to see the show and go to bed! I do go to bed earlier if he’s not on!” She sassed with such a cheek.

To which Stanley replied; “Well you won’t miss him when we don’t have a television; you’ll be too preoccupied! And you need your sleep tonight! Early rises tomorrow!” He pressed Sternly

Laura nearly snapped at him then but she realised its only a TV show and it wasn't worth it, her thyroid swelled up and she got a bit teary and spat it out; "I can't help it, the medicine makes me drowsy then wears off a little then kicks in again half an hour after I take it. I want to sleep but I can't! Every time I close my eyes my eyelids have to squeeze shut to stay that way and it gives me a head ache I get itchy on my skin during the night and a really blocked nose and a dry throat apart from that my eyes dash from one corner of their sockets to the other when ever they hear a noise and my muscles tense when ever you move!

How can I sleep through all that? I feel tireder every day! They should make medicine that doesn't have such crappy side effects. If sleep is so crucial why give out drugs that disrupt it?" She asked.

To which he replied; "Well, when they tested them they had more good results than bad, even if they stopped half from sleeping, they prevented most from having seizures, to an advisable extent. Enough to have them distributed anyway... These drugs were the only anti convulsants to ever come out. They are in a sense medi-evil, but better you start on something weaker if your going to build an immunity to anti convulsants, than start on the strongest newest medication! Other wise if you become immune to it first, there's nothing for you to change to or increase onto, and each newer anti convulsant has less likely but worse, if affected, side effects than the last! You have to think of beating and treating epilepsy like a game of chess! Use your pawns first, see how it reacts, stay one step ahead of the game from day 1!" Stanley explained.

"He had an answer for everything didn't he/ A game? A challenge? Easy for him to say he didn't have to experience the side effects! Did he? Did any of the doctors's try out the anti convulsants on themselves doubt it!" Thought Laura.

Laura frowned! She crossed her arms and stuck out her tongue and lifted her nose in the air. Stanly could see she was upset.

"Maybe one day there will be a treatment that has the opposite side effect! But for now we'll just have to wait!" He said as he smiled slunk next to her and put his arm around her. "Now come with me," he said kissing her hand softly,

"We've got to go and pick up the Chinese food we ordered. It should be ready by now!" Said Stanley ever so irresistibly, pulling her up off the couch and kissing her again. Nothing made Laura move better than Stanley's puppy dog eyes or food.

"All right, I'm coming!" She replied and off they went! As they pulled up outside the Chinese restaurant Stanley noticed he couldn't get a park, so he gave Laura a fifty;

"Go in, give them my name and pay, and I'll keep the car running." He said.

“Okay!” She replied, Laura was fast she jumped out went to the desk, did what he asked, and came back.

“Laura?” Stanley asked worried.

“Mm?” She replied with a sweet smile seemingly absent-minded.

“Where’s the food?” He asked smiling back like it was no big deal.

“Huh? Oh!” Laura freaked and ran back inside a little embarrassed. The clerk was holding it up. “Uh, thanks!" Blushed Laura.

Bye.” Said waving and ran back out to the car. The clerk shook his head, put his pencil back behind his ear, and went to take the next orders to the chef.

“Sorry Stanley.” She said with a pleading grin.

“Come on Laura; Let’s go home!” He said laughing and they drove off.

After dinner Stanley gave Laura a quarter of a sleeping pill he had.

“Take this now with lots of water don't do this every night but you might find you’d sleep better if you’ve already gotten some sleep in. And the reason you cant take these every night is because they are easy to get used to and need more of and then your brain becomes reliant on drug induced sleep and cant produce a natural sleep by itself. Okay?"

The next day Laura was packing when she got a terrible migraine and fell over. Stanley heard the noise from the bathroom and rushed to see what happened.

“Laura, what’s the matter?” He asked.

“I’ve got a headache, when I stood back up over the suit case to see how much space was left, everything went black and I fell over.” She explained; “can you get me some Panadol?”

As he opened the medicine draw he noticed it hadn't been packed up yet and there were two missed doses left in her pillbox.

“Laura, did you take your medicine today?” He asked. “Um, no? I guess not, I can’t actually remember!” She replied; “I’ll take it now!”

“No Laura you can't it’s 3:00pm if you do that you’ll just cause an overdose for later tonight. You’re just going to have to start again from tonight!” Worried Stanley.

“No I wont, I can just take the night-time dose later as well!” She said.

Stanley gave in he couldn’t risk her having a fit in the air! “Fine” he said; “But what about last nights dose it’s in here too!”

“No, I took last nights dose, I put that in there last night for tonight when you told me we were flying out in the evening just in case I had to take it on the plane or something. I don’t know how long it takes!” Explained Laura.

“Oh. Good. Here I’ll pack the rest of it now! You just take your pills and rest on the way there and just take it easy! It’s time to go now.” He said; “We should get to your mother’s house by nine pm.

“Yay!” Yelped Laura; “I hope we don’t scare her! Boy, won’t she be surprised!” Laughed Laura.

“I’m sure she’ll be delighted.” Smiled Stanley as he kissed her head.

“Let me just take the trunks down while you wait here and relax and then I’ll come back up and hel... I mean, *escort* you down the stairs my lady! Mwah!” He kissed her hand grinning as she gave him a suspicious stubborn look.

“I can get down the stairs myself!” She groaned.

“I know dear but you look a little faint right now and i don’t want to risk you falling! I guess this will teach you to take your medicine on time then, huh missy?” He taunted.

Laura folded her arms and stuck her nose up at him and gave a big “Humpf!”

But she couldn’t hold her anger over something so petty for long it became difficult to keep a straight face after a while. Her frown cracked, and turned into a giggle and a;

“Pff! Alright, I’ll wait but only because you're so charming and because you care, and I wouldn’t want to worry *you,* Stanley!” She smarted.

“You always worry me honey! Whether its because you don’t care about yourself enough or because you don’t know how to or are simply incapable, you worry me!” He laughed;

“I’ll be right back, I promise!” And off he went with the luggage.

And before Laura could finish her coke he was back ready to walk her down the stairs like a queen.

“That was quick!” She said.

Then she noticed out of her window the driver fitting the last of the luggage into the boot. She looked back at Stanley who was sporting a clever look on his face.

“Never mind.” She said, and got into the car.

She shuffled over to make room for Stanley and they cuddled all the way to the airport.

On the plane Laura began to look pasty, she started heaving and couldn’t stop so Stanley gave her some Maxillin.

“How do you feel? You don’t usually do this on the helicopter!” He asked concerned.

“I’ll be alright, my ears keep popping and I’ve got a headache my nose is blocked from the vomit and there's a lot of pressure in my eyes causing the headache. My head feels like it's got water in it my arms and legs are hurting and my chest is tight. My hands and feet have pins and needles sharp pins and needles and my face around my eyelids is twitching just here.” She pointed.

Stanley felt her face and checked her pulse. He tried to take her blood pressure but in doing so he ruptured a cluster of spider veins some recently new spider veins. It was obvious she had cabin fever,

"I know you're not supposed to take aspirin sweetie, but it can't do you any harm right now because your blood pressure is through the roof! If all it risks is lowering your blood pressure now is the best time for it!" Stanley said surely.

"Ok," she said; "lets try that."

The Aspirin brought her blood pressure down but not much so Stanley offered her some Valllium. It does the same thing but calms the nerves, anxiety and makes you drowsy, and... Vallium is also used as an emergency anti-convulsant during lengthy seizures.

Four minutes later Laura was out like a light, she was alive and snoring in fact jibbering in her sleep but well at least she wasn't sick.

Stanley checked her pulse again it was a little slower than usual so he checked her other obs and they were fine.

Although, he did need a wheelchair to get her off the plane when they touched down because she was so unsteady. But her mother's house was still two hours drive from the airport so Laura had plenty of time left to come to.

That girl, when she was in a deep sleep, she slept like a bump on a log! Even with all the bumps the car went over and the potholes she slept.

In the end Stanley did have to wake her up when they got there.

“Oh, where are we?” She asked confused.

“We’re here!” He said.

“You slept the whole way! Come on Let’s go and scare the shit out of your mother!” He joked.

“Yay!” She replied, still tired.

And they both headed for the house.

(TheOthers)

“Knock, knock!” They both called together. “Mummy? It’s Laura, I’m back! Hello?” Tried Laura.

The place went quiet, almost like the neighbours heard and were quietening down and starting to listen in. But then they heard slippers on the floor behind the door.

Suddenly the door opened, and a dark figure lifted up a carotene lamp and held it out to their faces wearily; “Laura? Is it really you, oh my dear look at you!” She

chuffed; “You’re all dolled up like a princess! My daughter the Marionette?” She giggled. Give me a hug, I missed you so much!” Continued the woman.

“And who’s this strong young man holding your bags?” She flirted.

Laura blushed and replied; “Um, this is Stanley! He's my fiance we’re getting married! He’s a doctor mum, he saved me!”

“Aah, yes? I’ve heard about you from the priests at the church. I asked how Laura was doing, and to my surprise he told me she was doing better and a doctor was looking after her.” Laura's mother explained.

“Oh, my dear sweet baby girl,” she started again and then realized why she was feeling a bit too chilly; “Oh! Sorry come in the two of you quickly please, goodness. It's late! I never thought I'd see you again baby after what you've been through and how you've been treated, I expected

you'd run away and never come back. I've never seen you so elated though, I must say! Look at you your glowing, you look so much more rested and radiant and happy! I'm so glad to see you're being taken care of.

I did hope you'd come back and visit me, my dear. The two of you must be dead tired! Have you eaten yet?" Asked Mummy flustered.

Her heart was racing. She was struggling to keep her train of thought, there were questions she wanted answers to...

But she was obviously still half-asleep herself! "Actually we had an in-flight meal; we took a fairly late flight because Laura seems to have trouble getting up in

the mornings." Smarted Stanley cheekily taunting Laura. But Mummy didn't quite catch the joke.

"Well It's about time she got some sleep. That girl could hardly have slept a full week in her life living here! I heard you're taking special medicine now that we don't have here. May I have a look?" Asked Mummy.

"Sure, I think it's about due to be taken now any way, if you get me some water mum and I'll show you." Offered Laura.

“Yes, of course... there you are sweetie, now show me how you take it!” She pushed.

“Like this mummy, I put this tablet in my mouth and wash it down with a drink (as long as it’s not alcohol though).” She demonstrated.

It was amazing that something so simple could have prevented everything!

“Very clever dear... Maybe you could share it with some of the elders and the younger mothers? Their babies are sick too. She asked curiously.

“Um, no mum, everyone’s different! I can’t share my

medication with them it might not suit them!” Laura explained.

“I think Doctor Stanley could pay them a visit in the morning though” she yawned; “but for now, bed time?” Laura asked hopefully.

“Of course dear, how long are you staying? Asked her mother.

“Well you don't have to worry about us leaving too soon. After breakfast Stan and I could re arrange the furniture in the lounge, and you could go and spread the word that he’s here. And if they’re sick to come and see him?” Replied Laura

To which Stanley added; “Yes, I have some emergency supplies and I may be able to order in some medication and machines to diagnose each of them properly. If you like?”

“Oh yes, I think that's a great idea you two! Every one will be so grateful, I bet. Oh your such a good girl, and you, oh what a nice boy! Good night you two, you can take my room. The bed is bigger and I’ve been sleeping in Laura's bed ever since the church took her from me so I’ll sleep there! I’ve really missed you Laura, I’m so happy you’re back we have so much to catch up on! I will make it up to you my dear. Thankyou so much for saving her Doctor Stanley.”

She was getting too emotional now; “Good night!” She finally finished.

“Good night mummy.” Said Laura and kissed her cheek. “Good night Mrs...” Stan began, but was stopped by mummy.

“Please Stanley, call me mum or Glow!” She insisted “Okay! Goodnight Glow!” Replied Stanley smiling.

After she closed the door behind her, Stanley and Laura looked at each other worried.

“Go to sleep Laura, I’ve just got to hook up the computer.” He said.

“Please don’t stay up for too long Stanley it sounds like a full day of work tomorrow!” Laura begged.

“No worries love, it’ll just take a few minutes.” Replied Stanley.

“Okay” said Laura; “Good night.

“Good night Laura!” Said Stan as he kissed her on the lips. And he started setting up.

THE POOR HOSPITAL

At four O'clock in the morning, Laura awoke to banging and nocking and scraping noises. She went to put her hand on Stanley to wake him, but he was missing.

She crept out of her bedroom and peered out through the hallway. She noticed all the lights were on downstairs and the lounge room was filled with hospital machines.

"I must be dreaming?" She thought.

Then she noticed Stanley guiding two guys in, who were carrying boxes. Stanley's friends had come straight down and donated some of their outdated machines and were helping him to hook them up!

"Wow!" exclaimed Laura; "are you serious? What's going on?" She asked.

"Isn't it obvious?" Replied Stanley; "we are setting up diagnostics! Tomorrow we're renovating the backyard to take beds, and we're going to build a Chemistry Lab to make up and store all the medicines in." He continued.

It's not illegal to do that here and if it's held here it can be prescribed given and administered here.

The people won't need to pay, but the community can donate their old blankets and any harvestables or food they decide they don't need to keep it going.

Its going to be a community owned and founded poor hospital.

I've already taken care of the legal stuff. And your mother has agreed to help out. In fact it was her Idea to transform the cottage into a hospital." Explained Stanley. "Now try to go back to sleep if you can? I'm sorry we woke you up, but we're almost done! We just have to

rearrange the lounges and coffee table. I'll be back up in a

minute, I promise!" Said Stanley.

"But what about your friends were will they sleep?" Asked Laura.

"Doctor Carey, and Professor Newbert? They're staying at the Motel in town, it's three minutes drive from here1 don't worry about them, they can take care of themselves!" Joked Stanley.

"We most certainly can!" Said Newbert; "isn't that right Carey?" He proclaimed

"Aye miss, tis true! You go on back to bed and wait for your Stanley my dear; we'll be alright!" Confirmed Carey. Laura liked doctor Carey she thought he had a cheeky accent. Every word he said seemed genuine but at the same time it was so hard not to giggle when he spoke. He was like a leprechaun but taller, and she couldn't stop trying to imagine him in a pirate hat.

"Okay, goodnight gentlemen!" She said as she smiled wryly with her brows raised, making a conscious effort every other second not to laugh. She rolled her eyes to the left then turned her head and then quickly one-eightied the rest of her body to follow and walked back to the bedroom dragging her fingers against the wall to hide her haste to hide and crack up laughing.

The then she calmed down and climbed back under the blankets and went to bed.

The next morning Glow burst into their bedroom; "It's time, they're starting to arrive! I'm going back down stairs to make the lemonade!" She said and as fast as she burst in she left in a flash.

Stan and Laura looked at each other... "Time to get up?"

Asked Laura and Stan nodded. "Let's get dressed quickly!" He said.

Laura put on her dress and sandals and ran down to help her mother. Trying to tie the neck straps on her dress on the way down the stairs, stupidly, she twisted her ankle on the second last step, as the morning light coming in through the window struck her retina!

She was okay, just a bruise here, and a scrape on her palms and one of her knees. Laura was rendered useless for the day drinking juice and icing her ankle with a block of frozen mince.

“Take care of that!” Said Glow, trying to hide her concern and automated stress sarcastically; “It’s what’s for dinner you know? Tacos! So, don’t let it defrost completely on your ankle or we will be eating off the floor!” She laughed.

“Mmhm” replied Laura unamused; “Don’t fuss too much mum Stan will have something to bring the swelling down I wont need the mince for too long!”

Just then Stanley walked around the corner and into the kitchen staring at and trying to fix his tie. “Okay, nearly done,” he started slowly but as he looked up! His jaw dropped in shock when he seen Laura; “Huh, what happened?” He asked.

“Well I don’t know, I was rushing down the Stairs tying my dress, then the sun flashed me in the eyes, and I freaked a bit because I couldn’t see and I twisted my ankle. I guess. I’ll be fine though wont I? It’ll go down?” Replied Laura.

“Of course, I’ve got a cold pack and a bandage and I might test your blood levels too! But after we’re done with everyone else, I think we should do an EEG on you too!

That way we’ll be able to tell if your getting worse and your meds aren’t working or if the meds are working and you’re forgetting to take them is causing it. Okay Hun?”

He said in a lecturing but sexy super caring tone, which made Laura blush.

“Okay!” She answered as he started bandaging her ankle. Then he took her blood and put her on desk duty.

“So, what do I have to do?” She asked.

To which he replied, "Just write down their names as they come in, one after the other in the form of a list. I’ll check the list, call a name, make them a file and bring it out to you after to put away. Then you schedule their next appointment with them in this diary here. And If I tell you to, take them to a bed with their file and make them comfortable. Hang that file at the foot of the bed, and write the bed's number on the front of the file with black marker also, so they don’t get switched by accident. And because some patients get confused and hop into other people's beds." He jested.

"Once you’ve bedded a patient make sure you get their next of kin and that address in case of an emergency, so that they can be notified. Glow can help you with bedding the patients and serving them drinks. Don’t forget to serve the patients waiting because it can take a while to diagnose each patient and decide what to do with them and we don’t need anybody dehydrating or getting heat stroke. And Glow?” He added.

“Check their files for special notes towards current triggers like dehydration or lights for example make sure you keep offering them water or in the case of lights keep their curtains closed where the light might come in but don't forget to check on them! My sister will be here soon she's a nurse she's going to help with the scans teach you how to check their obs and blood pressure and how to take their blood. Okay girls?" He asked, finally finished.

"Got it!" They answered together.

"Okay Glow! Let them in!" He said. Glow nodded and went to the door, a group were sitting shaded against the front wall of the house waiting. The elders, as they were known came in one at a time and upon Glows instructions took off their hats and walked into the kitchen, lined up and one by one gave their names to Laura. A girl they knew almost five years ago Satins future wife. Now they too suffered as they had developed epilepsy with old age shortly after Laura left the Asylum.

Please take a seat and the doctor will be with you shortly!" Said Laura blushing, as she tried to sound very professional, something that was too easy but felt stupid. It was fun however the more she said it the more confident she felt.

"Thanks there missy," said Marve in his huffy voice. Marve was the eldest and was the closest of the group of elders to Laura's late grandfather.

He was her favourite so far.

Some more people arrived, they were mostly kids and one woman. Two of her kids, the youngest, the twins, were sick! Their names were Penny and Poko, Laura felt connected to them and sorry for them too, she didn't want them to suffer like she did, but she managed to keep it together by repeating to herself quietly; "It could have been allot worse at least they can start treatment early".

Stanley also had asked them to stay over night for a few more tests and monitoring children were much more difficult to treat.

Marve had his blood taken and had an EEG and was

given follow up appointments. The rest of the elders were to come back tomorrow afternoon for more tests, they didn't seem to have epilepsy but they definitely had bad cholesterol high sensitivity to light and heart problems.

Stan needed to find out if it was just their hearts or if they had tumours or something. Their so-called seizures seemed more like mini strokes!

"Too much tobacco, and too much beer!" Stanley warned them. They Laughed.

"Okay," he said; "just have to finish testing the kids now and monitor them overnight, and I'll know what to give them and they can go home. I'll call the boys in! Oh, is gabby here yet?" He asked.

"Not yet!" Said Laura; "it's only 2:30pm she doesn't get here until 3:00pm" She reminded him.

"Is that all?" Stanley asked Glow; "No one else?" He asked.

"Um, yes" replied Glow; "for now anyway the priests are coming by with some of their patients after siesta though!" She replied.

"Okay, so there's time for a breather and a break girls." He said; "well done!" He congratulated them.

"Actually he said, in that case don't worry about the over night thing I can monitor he kids during siesta, and they'll be home in time for dinner!"

When gabby gets here with the Pharmaceutical team I should have their meds maid up and ready for pick up before bed, Marve's too." He said.

"That's great!" Said Laura; "mum, can you go and inform the families of the good news?"

"It would be my pleasure!" Said Glow. And She put on her hat and her shoes and left.

THE FIRST PHARMACY

Gabby showed up at a quarter past four with the pharmaceutical team.

"Okay Gab Set it up in the upstairs bathroom for now." Said Stanley; "then come and take the patients blood pressures!"

"Okay, Stan!" Gabby replied, then she stopped and looked around and asked; "Where are *your* friends?"

Laura answered for him like a know it all: "Outside extending the ward and creating a better place to mix up the medicines!"

Gabby giggled; "You mean make up the meds, if you tell people we've been mixing up the meds you'll cause a panic! Silly." She said.

Laura blushed and shrugged.

The priests dropped in, but they only had two patients who weren't responding to the power of god.

Stanley thanked them on behalf of the patients for bringing them and invited them to leave.

Laura got their names, "Franklin, and Percy? You can stay tonight, once we get you sorted you can go back to your real homes with your new medications. And attempt to start a new life without persecution, provided you keep taking your medicine as instructed and keep your appointments, in case the medication starts to wear off.

It'll take two weeks to start making any noticeable effect, maybe a little less. it wont fix strait away so keep rested if your still having any siezures after the dose may not be high enough. Don't increase it by yourself it's too dangerous. Come back in and we'll advise you how to step it up. Let us know if your worried if you feel twitchy or shakey or too tired or unwell in any way!

But first thing is first, and that is EEG's! Also we are having tacos tonight for dinner, and are either of you thirsty?" She finished.

They both nodded, with in a half minute of sitting down they had drunk the entire pitcher of lemonade between them.

"Okay?" thought Laura, "I'll get mum to make some more and lay out some sandwiches before you two decide to eat the furniture!"

"Mum?" She called.

Glow ran in; "Yes dear?" she replied.

"Mummy, these guys are famished, can you make some more lemonade and some sandwiches?" Asked Laura.

"Well, the lemonade takes a while, so you start making the sandwiches and I'll get started on the lemonade." Replied Glow.

Laura looked at the boys and raised an eye brow, as if to ask "think you can hold out for two more minutes?" The guys looked at each other and nodded. Once done Laura took the sandwiches to the table and sat down with the boys while they ate.

Suddenly out of nowhere it happened! There seemed to be no warning and no trigger. Laura fell backwards on her chair. She'd gone completely out of control.

It started with a yelp and an arch. Her legs twisting, caught in her chair.

She was so contorted, she looked like she was convulsing in a head stand position! Her eyes rolled into the back of her head.

Blood started to froth out of her mouth.

The two boys tried to help move her but it was for nort!

They couldn't lift her heavy stiff contorted convulsing frame. She was too caught, stuck! One leg wedged under a chair leg the other hanging over the seat of the chair hooked around the chairs front leg.

It was a nightmare! Two minutes went past and she was still going! Glow was screaming hysterically, Gabby heard and ran in, and strait back out, fifteen seconds later she came bolting back in with Stanley, Carey and Newbert.

Gabby rummaged through Stan's emergency bag Grabbed the Maxillin and squeezed it into Laura's mouth, after a few seconds the frothing slowed.

And Laura's abdomen stopped throwing itself, but her back was still arched, and her body tense. She was still seizing but maybe she'd be easier to move.

The grabbed her legs, and everyone helped turn her, Carey grabbed the Chair and said; "okay, Lift and untangle the top leg!Good lift her hips as i lift the chair! Ready? Go!". Carey pulled the cahir away and put it out of the way.

Stanley grabbed some Vallium; "Hold her steady," he said as he extracted the dosage "I'm going to put it in her left arm, the one she's lying on, if you can keep her from

rolling onto it, it'll work!"

"Okay, hold her, hold, Hold, HOLD!" he removed the syrringe from her arm adn exhaled; "Okay, let her go!" he said.

It took a couple of seconds, but she slowly went limp. She didn't wake up, though this was to be expected. At least now, she was breathing again.

Laura slept for two days before her hunger got the better of her and woke her up. Man, was she sore.

most of all in her head neck and her leg!

"What happened? I feel like I was hit with a tone of bricks! Where am I? Stanley?" she searched.

Laura looked around and the room started spinning. "Stanley?" she screamed.

Suddenly she heard some thumping sounds getting closer. Stanley opened the door and the ligt shone through it! He rushed to her side and embraced her.

Laura looked over his shoulder and saw Gabby and Glow in the door way and it hit her, She *was* at home, sort of.

She was in Glows room.

"What happened? How did I get here?" she asked him.

Laura couldn't remember the trip down or the first day or the hospittal idea or the patients! She didn't know what day or time it was.

She'd lost some short term memory, she'd developed a little amnesia!

"Are you hungry?" Glow asked.

"Yes but, ouch I don't know if I *can* eat." She replied. "you've been asleep for days Laura, you need to try!" said Gabby.

Laura weeped a bit and said, "It hurts soo much!" "Where?" asked Stanley.

"Everywhere!" she replied; "My whole body! My head, and my mouth, my leg and my ankle. my tummy my neck my throat! My mouth!" She stuck out her swollen tongue. "Well we'll have to dress that! Looks like you might need to stick to smoothies and chilled soup. Can you move?" He asked.

Laura tried and burst into tears. “No!” She cried; “it hurts too much!”

Stanley put some morphene into her canula. “Okay, your eating in here then!” he said.

Laura whispered into his ear, “I need to go to the toilet!” Stanley laughed a bit; “That’s okay, just go we’ve got you hooked up to some waste bags. I’ll get Gabby to swap them out when your finished. You can go to the toilet when you can move!”

Laura looked confused, she looked under the blanket and went pale, “That’s desgusting!” She said.

She felt as if her dignity just went out the window.

Gabby came over to her side and said, “It’s alright, I don’t mind, besides you were going to do it whether you woke up or not.

“Eeew!” said Laura. “Gab can we take these off first, so I can go the normal way then you just have to walk me in. I know he means well but I don’t think Stan realizes how indignifying it feels to consiously go to the toilet in a couple of bags full of shit and piss sitting on your stomach.”

“Okay, since you put it that way, Are you sure you can hold onto it while I unhook you?” she replied “Definately!” Laura assured.

After they came back from the bathroom, Gabby busted; “I’ll bring you back up to speed tomorrow okay? I don’t want you to worry about it for now!”

she explained.

“Okay?” Replied Laura... Bad choice of words!

THE WEDDING

The next morning Laura's memory returned, and she remembered why they were there. But not how *it* happened.

Gabby told her that they were almost finnished with the hospital when Laura had her seizure. And while Laura was asleep they completed it and the pharmacy, and brought in qualified chemists to run it.

"Well, that didn't take long! We must have had alot of help!" Said Laura.

"That's not the best part though!" Gabby replied;

"Stanley told everyone you were having the wedding here! It got everyone motivated. And the hospitals getting some decent media coverage, we've even set up a public hospital fund so complete strangers can donate to the cause. And the government because of the coverage, have announced a plan to help fund the hospital. theyre offering more pharmacies and calsses for G.P's on Epilepsy. there should be fifteen more pharmacies in fifteen suburbs by next year."

"You don't have to say much if the media try to talk to you, stanley's already spilled just say thanks and things like that! Oh, and I tested the urine sample you gave me when you woke up last night!

Laura, you're pregnant! thats why you had the fit, your weight metabolism and circulation have changed. So some of the medicine is going to the baby!" she finished.

"I'm going to be a mummy?" asked Laura.

"Yes!" Gabby replied; "But It's complicated! If your medicine is too high it could kill the baby if it's not high enough your seizures will kill the baby! and your medicine is not up high enough to fully control your fits, but if w put it up it could cause the baby damage or kill it!

So, you're going to have to really take care of yourself, I mean nurse your self! No stress, no worrying, no getting too excited, no bees in your bonnet. Okay, Laura?

If you're concerned or worried or want something, we will help you. You have to put your pride aside and accept that if you dont let us help you, you'll be putting the baby at risk, not just yourself!

If you get bored we can go shopping or something out of the ordinary but you have to take it easy and not push yourself. Eye patches, sunglasses hats!" Gabby explained. "But why do my siezures affect the baby Gabby?" Laura asked.

"Because," gabby explained "you stop breathing for long periods of time if you cant breath the baby cant! And as for every other part of your seizures, they're violent and dangerous. would you throw yourself down the stairs pregnant? Would you punch a pregnant person in the uterus?" she asked.

Laura felt depressed, "So no matter what I do, whether I kill it or have it, it's going to be worser off, or wish it were dead!" She sobbed

"No Laura! There's more to life than sick and healthy, happy or sad! Even if *you* feel like your illness effects their quality of life, *they* wont! You would be their whole life, they'd look to you for strength for character, perspective, help, love. Even the most horribly treated child would love their parents. You will be a wonderful mum Laura, because you know how it feels to be treated differently and you'll be a warrior for their souls even after you die!

The child will love you, cherish you, call your name when it hurts itself or teeths or is scared or hungry!

Don't think on it so much now, you're getting married and starting a family! Soo many people love and appreciate you around here already Laura! You're the best thing that could have happened to them, your a beautiful daughter and your going to be a beautiful wife and mother, your giving me the gift of a sister , and to others friendship.

You've brought the locals here, treatment, answers, and hope!" Concluded Gabby.

"Also," she said; "Stanley has been in conference all morning, there is some new research being conducted, new medications being trialled, he's trying to get approvals for trials here. None of them have been proven onehundred percent side effect proof and none of them deemd safe for pregnancy. So you have to wait until after the pregnancy.

Even if the disease were isolated to one part of your brain it would be too dangerous to operate on someone who is pregnant!" She said.

"Oh, and I heard, they are looking at an invasive surgery

where they put a big computer in the side of your head and wire it into your brain. but it looks too groussem, and their is a pace maker for the brain, less invasive they just wire it to a nerve in your neck and it sends electric signals to hush your braincells. It doesn't hurt but stanley wont

considder it unless the medications don't work.There is soo much hope for you Laura. Your could live to be a great grandma. The others, I'm not so sure about because most of the approved trials are legal in other countries but probably wont be legal here yet for another five years.

Where as you and Stan can travel. but maybe we can figure something out for the others. Epilepsy research isn't really top priority when it comes to approving trials here and some other countries. You, Stanley and the kids may be fighting for epilepsy awareness for years!" She finished. Laura rolled over in her pillow and screamed!

It was at this point gabby realised herself that there were just some things she needed to keep from Laura.

"Forget that, Laura. It's so far away. Lets just focus on now, okay. Don't be discouraged. You've got the rest of your life to worry about that stuff. There are two wonderful things happening right now. Any woman would kill to be you, sick or not!" Said Gabby.

“So Laura, ‘first thing’s first’,” came a voice so harmonious as it walked through the door.

It was Stanley; “Public or private?” He asked.

Laura thought a moment, and considered what Gabby said about too much excitement, and taking it easy, and then replied in certainty: “Private!”

Gabby walked out and stood hanging out the doorway, she seemed to be talking to somebody.

That somebody was the towns preacher. He walked to the

end of the bed.

“What’s this?” Laura asked... Then gabby and Glow walked in and stood in the back corners of the bedroom. “This is it, Laura!” whispered Stanley. And he shuffled side ways onto the bed beside Laura. He held her hand and stared deeply into her eyes, preening in glory the whole time knowing he was making her blush.

And the minister began, “Dearly beloved we are gathered in this bedroom today, to witness the marriage of these two young people who are entering into their sacred bond and exchanging their vows, before family, and before god!” He preached.

“Do you Stanley take Laura to be your lawfully wedded wife, to have and to hold, to love and to cherrish, in sickness and in health, and foresaking all others promise to love honour and protect her as long as you both shall live?" Asked the priest.

Stanley said, "I do!"

Stanley smiled and Laura blushed deeper. This was now though, a staring competition, Laura felt she would lose!

"And do you Laura, take Stanley to be your lawfully wedded husband, to have and to hold, to love and to cherish, in sickness and in health, and forsaking all others, promise to love honor and protect him, as long as you both shall live?"

"I Do!" Replied Laura.

Laura cracked the biggest cheesy grin, and giggled, then tried to hide it, by pursing her lips together like she'd just sucked on a lemon. Then her mouth and lips got tired fast and she was soon half smiling again and biting her lip.

"I know pronounce you husband and wife! You may kiss the bride... after you give her the ring that is!"

said the priest.

Laura's smile widened as she wrapped her arms around her new husband's neck craving his lips like a mad woman. And Stanley kissed her, he fell right into that one! Glow and Gabby blushed they quickly left and shut the door!

"I love you Laura!" Stanley whispered. And she melted all her previous worries a distant memory.

"I love you too!" She replied.

Then he layed her down and lifted her gown.

“And I love you too, little baby!” He kissed her belly, repeatedly , and it tickled, so bad!

Laura giggled joyfully, then lye still cuddling into stanleys chest. Playing with his chest hair and started pondering deep thought again.

The wedding was so short and sudden and surprising, she felt over the moon, so different to how she felt before. She thought, “maybe I’m going mental!”

At that moment Stan noticed her mood change and replied as if he’d read here mind or she’d spoken outluod. Maybe she had.

Your not crazy Laura, you’re pregnant! your mood is as vulnerable and impressionable as an exposed nerve.” He explained.

“Come on, get dressed. we are going shopping.” Laura got excited and then thought about Gabby. Her eyes flashed toward the door.

“Don’t worry about Gabby, it’s just you and me today!” he explained. But how did he know?

Laura smiled, Stanley had just thrown a very pretty dress on the bed, she’d never seen before. gosh she was spoiled.

“This is our special day! here let me help.” He said.

He started undressing her and well... what would you have done?

PREGNANT

It was week eighteen and everything was going well-ish. Laura had two more seizures, but the baby's growth remained healthy it seemed.

Question was why was she fitting again after they'd been so careful? That was something they couldn't understand. Anyway, today was to Laura, the day she got to find out if it were a boy or a girl. The baby seemed to be asleep for now.

Laura was bigger than she ought to have been, and when the ultra sound started there was a kick. Suddenly there were three feet on the screen.

Surely they were seeing things?

The sonographer decided to go long... one, two three, four legs in one sack, two visible umbilical chords.

Twenty fingers, twenty toes, two heads two rows of pearls, the sonographer checked to make sure they weren't' conjoined. As she prodded one of them tumbled one way and the other turned upside down. Okay they aren't joined. And now the sex... Two boys.

Wow so the good news was she was having two beautiful boys, the bad news was double trouble...

Laura needed to be way more vigilant and aware of what was happening inside of her. There were two active flipping kids inside her sharing a room both with there own bungee chord attached to a shared placenta, and so the fear was entanglement.

She was given a card to call any time she felt pain, to check on the babies as being twins there was an increased likeliness of an early delivery.

The first thing Laura did was buy some boy clothes, blue was okay but she wanted bright pictures and cute speech bubbles too. Two of everything, in premmie, in newborn, and in three months size just incase.

And she got it all of it delivered and set up for her.

They had their own cottage by the beach now, they moved in the day they got married! Laura thought back to when Stanley threw the pretty dress on the bed and helped her get undressed.

"Rotten little sneak!" She murmured as she watched him set up one of the bassinets.

She sat down on the rocking chair, petting their little

blankets and then remembered the clothes she just bought still needed to be folded and put away.

This made her happy! She grabbed a shopping bag and started unpacking it, pulling the price tags off, checking the sizes and even though she'd just spent hours doing it in the shops held each item and its twin against her belly before folding.

Side by side, up right side ways, upside down one up one down. Every now and again dragging her fingers along her abdomen.

She was utterly infatuated by what was happening, ultimately obsessed, self-amused and very quiet. Although every now and then she'd giggle and wipe a tear from hear eye. Stanley looked up.

Goodness knows what was going on inside her head at that point, he thought.

She glanced up at Stanley and thought she must look a loon, and she laughed again.

She knew how crazy she looked, and was acting. She imagined how she would look to someone else, and that only amused her more. She folded the clothes and went to put them away.

As she got up, the room started to spin and she lost her balance. She caught herself on a chest of draws and started trembling.

Stanley stopped what he was doing and jumped up to her side immediately and held her close. He walked her over to the bed and laid her down and put an oxygen mask on her face. He could feel her burning up, so he grabbed her a cold flannel, a glass of water and some paracetamol.

"Are you alright? How do you feel? Are you in pain? Does your belly hurt Laura?" He rambled on worried.

“No, my belly is fine!” She said, “I was walking and the room spun around all the sudden! She explained.

“I’d say so!” He replied, “you’ve got a scorching fever!” He went on

Laura fluttered her eyes and twitched a little.

“You need a nap!” Said Stanley sternly, “You've been on your feet all day in this heat!” Put on you’re eye patch!” “okay.” She said.

He checked her lips and her mouth. “You’re dehydrated!” He stated, “I’m going to get you a drip so you can sleep while you’re rehydrating, drink some water for now.

Stanley came back and attached a damned catheter to her hand!

“Ouch!” She cried.

“Big baby!” Remarked Stanley with a cheek.

“Humpf, how rude!” Replied Laura, “How would you like it if someone put a sharp stick in your arm every time you got sick?”

“You’re right! I suppose I’d be sick of it by now too!” He said in a coy way.

“I suppose I should be used to it by now?” Said Laura, rolling her eyes, half upset. “At least it’s you doing it Stanley, and not some one else.” She tried to smile as he attached the sodium chloride bag to the hanger.

“There you are, all done! He proclaimed. “Now, have a nap! Ill be in the nursery if you need me. I’m going to shut the door to give you some peace and quiet, but I'm switching on the baby monitor so I can hear if something happens, Okay?”

“Okay, baby!”

Sure enough she became rehydrated and her fever reduced. A sudden feeling of coldness in her arm and

drowsiness and relaxedness hit and so after half an hour of trying to, she finally fell asleep.

Nineteen weeks later, Laura was sitting relaxing on a day bed on the beach with Gabby, under an umbrella juice in one hand, Gabby squirting sun cream into her other. And it happened.

Laura threw her drink, glass and all up in the air, just out of the blue and started jerking her arms violently. Slinging sun block, hitting herself in the chest and face, bashing the back of her head into the headrest on the chair. She arched up and rolled.

It all happened so fast that the glass she threw up came down heavy and hit her in the tummy as she fell off the chair. There was nothing anyone could do.

They were alone.

Gabby called out and no one heard. She searched her beach bag, no meds. And her mobile got no reception. She ran to Laura and held her head off of the sand, and dragged her into her arms.

Panicking wasn't helping. She rocked back and forward racking her mind trying to sooth her saying "Ssh, Ssh."

Then she spotted Laura's towel. She pulled it off the chair and draped it over Laura's eyes and then she remembered her own towel!

Quickly and carefully she laid Laura down on the towel, on the sand. She got, grabbed her own, raced down to the waters edge to saturate it and raced back.

When she got back she sat the wet towel on the chair picked up Laura again and wrung the wet towel over Laura's scalp. She wiped it over her face, her arms, chest neck and shoved it under Laura's back.

After about thirty seconds, Laura slowed down. Her skin got cooler! And Gabby kept repeating, "it's alright Laura, it's alright!"

THE BIRTH

Suddenly, Laura screamed in agony! Clawing at her stomach, and pushed of the ground with her toes for about thirty seconds, it lasted.

Before she stopped Gabby felt her own knees become drenched in warm water. Then Laura stopped screaming enough to catch her breath. Wondering what just happened.

Gabby thought out loud, "Please tell me you just peed on me?"

Laura heard and replied, "No, I didn't!" She said puffing wearily.

"Oh no!" Exclaimed gabby.

"Oh no!" Panicked Laura, knowing full well what that meant!

"Come on, get up! We've got to go NOW!" Said gabby. "Aaarrg!" Screamed Laura, crippled by pain, now on all fours!

Gabby pulled her up and helped her off the beach. Five minutes passed and they were only half way back to the cottage. Laura was dragging the chain, her contractions every thirty seconds, and the pressure on her cervix, felt like some one was shoving a stake up her, and no matter how much she kicked off the ground or tried to get off the ground that stake wasn't going anywhere!

Seven minutes later and they finally reached the cottage. Laura in agony on the floor waited while gabby called the emergency number on the fridge,

Within ten minutes a helicopter arrived on the beach. It took them a total of three minutes to get to Laura they

made a brace with their arms for her to sit on. She put her arms around them and they rushed her back to the helicopter, by which time Stanley arrived home to see and quickly got on the chopper. Boy was she happy to see him!

They reached the hospital in the closet city. But the facts turned out, yes her waters were broken but there was no body on the way out. The loaded her with morphine and gave her a C-section. They managed to get the boys out safely.

Obviously because they were twins, they were small, they were early. But to everyone's surprise there was also a third baby hiding behind the boys, a baby girl.

"Holy Crap, we're going to need another bassinet and some girls clothes!" Said Stanley.

"What?" Said Laura.

"Three!" Replied Stanley and she smiled.

LIFE WITH LITTLE ONES

The babies were required to stay in hospital for monitoring. Laura couldn't breastfeed, so they drank formula. But boy were they gutses.

They drank so much formula that they were released a week later. However they didn't reach newborn size for a month.

Not too shabby though!

It was hard with three kids. Three to feed, three to burp, three to change. Three to bathe, and three to put to bed! And of course the most heart aching three to teeth! But Laura got all the help she needed.

After the pregnancy Laura's medication was played with some more, with little success. Finally they switched her to a medication called Keppra. This seemed to control her grand mal siezures a lot better than epilem, nothing else worked at all.

They put her on Diamox for her migraines and to help control her partials. No matter what they tried there wasn't an hour still that she went without a partial. But at this moment they were better than Grandmals.

When the kids were one year old Laura had a Grandmal Seizure and after wards had to be reminded she ever had children.

When they were two and a half she had a cluster of Grandmal seizures, which started in the shower. And so her medication was pushed up.

When the kids were three, the family caught gastro from playgroup, this stress and dehydration had Laura fitting for a day and a half.

By the time they were starting preschool Laura was struggling to remember anything. Her life, her kids personalities, everything! They had her grandmals back under control for over a year, but her partials... They were affecting her badly.

They were ruining her life, at any time she could have up to thirty mall seizures in under an hour. The longest she went without having them was merely hours!

The doctors described it to her like this... "Listen Laura you're not going demented, It's what we call short-term memory loss. Say you remind yourself to do something or go to do something and before the paint has a chance to dry it gets washed off ."

Laura mentioned VNS because it was on the news.

But the doctors weren't keen on it because there was no explaining why it works.

"Keep to the meds... Try this... Try that! If it works good, if you have a fit it doesn't mean the meds aren't working. If it doesn't work, too bad you'll just have to wait until something new comes out."

How depressing and hypocritical. The VNS had the same chances as the medications of working and can be used with medications to stop things medications can't control.

Is natural and completely reversible why not try everything? Why don't they get it?

Later Laura discovered her Grandfather on her father's side and his sister who both lived in America, were both diagnosed with epilepsy, at different stages of life. They both died after developing Parkinson's and Alzheimer's. Her grandfather's sister diagnosed younger and died mid life. Her grandfather diagnosed in his old age and died shortly after diagnosis.

She worried. She worried for herself, for her family, for Stanley. For her kids, for their losses and how they would deal with it, and she worried for her future grandchildren. She told herself, "Next time I visit the doctor, I'm not taking no for an answer!"

And she didn't, she got the VNS four months later. It took a few months to take effect. But when it did, she stopped having partials.

She could look back and remember more than just things she memorized, the stories she told to her kids over and over, the names of the people she saw over and over.

She remembered everything that happened yesterday. Every thing she said, talked about, thought, felt, did.

Every person she talked to that day, what they said, what they did, how they reacted. She remembered clearly. And her children, their smiles, their laughs, the order they came in, each little expression of content, love cheek, appreciation, disappointment, every reaction.

She remembered their lunches, their bedtime, their bath time, and their dinnertime. Each ones time between toilet breaks.

She felt happy. Unbelievably happy. When they fought she appreciated it, when they made up, she felt proud.

When they showed their different cheeky personalities she would run over and tickle them to death.

She could do everything now. She watched them without help. She got a driver's license. She became independent. She helped at the hospital when they were at school. And when the family caught a virus she was only affected as much as the rest of them.

Laura was a new woman. An independent free spirit. She'd been given a second chance at life it seemed.

She could be who ever she wanted to be and do what she liked. She was reborn!

Rapid Neurological Decline

Twenty years on, twenty years of freedom and independence later, Laura woke up one morning covered in slime. So she slipped out of bed and went to the mirror. She noticed one half of her face had gone completely slack and she was helplessly drooling. She couldn't correct it, so she tried to move it with her hand. And she realised she couldn't move that arm.

She showed Stanley and he took her to the hospital. But she had no broken bones.

They did a few more scans on her and found out a part of her brain had stooped responding, had become inactive, had in a sense died.

They ran some more tests. An MRI of her brain showed up a Severe demyelination and age inappropriate white matter disease indicative of early onset Parkinson's Disease or dementia. The doctors started testing her blood for inflammatory and mitochondrial diseases. The biggest suspects being MS and MERRF Syndrome, so she had to send of a muscle biopsy as well.

After two more months she had lost control of one half of her body. The disease was advancing, the cause remained undefined. In just two days now it would be her birthday, and she would be forty-eight. She didn't want the kids to see her like this.

"They already know Laura, I told them. They will come and see you; you can't deny them that on pride, or out of fear for them, they're worried they haven't got much time left with you. You're not getting any better Laura. Now is as better time as any!

Let them see you, please?"

"Fine!" She snapped.

In the next two months Laura had lost function of her memory, she didn't know anyone. She didn't know Stanley or herself!

She became irritable. Eventually she was hospitalized, as the only parts left that functioned was her heart, her ears, and her frontal lobe (her emotions). She was put on a breathing machine and looked like she was sleeping.

Stanley, Glow, Gabby, and the kids, all grown up waited in her room silently. Taking turns kissing her and holding her hand and talking to her hoping something they said would trigger an emotional response. And for a while it did, then one night when everyone had gone but Stanley, while Stanley was speaking to her... Her heart stopped responding to his voice. And only fifteen seconds after, the lines on her observations monitor all went flat with an ear piercing…

“Boooooooooooop!”

Stanley pressed the emergency call button and screamed. The nurses rushed in and tried to restart her heart, but it didn’t work.

Laura was dead!

Stanley threw himself over her crying! Begging her, “No Laura, NO! NO baby! Please don’t leave me! Come back!” He screamed, “Please-!”

The nurse called the time. "January 6 10:45pm"

Stanley looked at them in disbelieve. “No that can’t be it, please. Keep trying!” He begged.

They all apologized, and one of them hugged him.

“It’s over mate, she’s gone. There’s nothing you can do now, she’s in a better place. Say your last goodbyes while you’ve got the time, the coroner will be here soon.” Said the nurse with the weird Australian accent, the one who said she was dead.

Stanley let go of her! He processed what the weird nurse had said and ran back over to the bed crying.

He stroked Lauras cheeks and sobbed, petting her hair as he wept. He kissed her eyelids, he kissed her nose. He whispered in her ear, “I love you!”

And he kissed her lips.

He sat down on the chair holding her hand gutted. The coroner came in and unhooked her, lifted her blanket to tag her. Stanley couldn't believe she was leaving. He took the opportunity to remember the smaller things. He went to the corner and held her tiny ankle, felt her feet and held her toes for a moment her cute little toes. He wiped his eyes with his sleeve. Then he left. Trying to hold his chin up. To be proud like her. He couldn't fathom how she managed it!

He cried again and called up the family to tell them. He held the phone to his face and noticed his wedding ring. Wiped his eyes and whispered. I will never forget you!

REMEMBERING LAURA

At the funeral everyone took turns remembering Laura, In front of the town and the press. Starting with Laura's mother Glow, and then Franklin, one of her patients with whom she went to school with.

Gabby talked about her first day working in the hospital. And her children reminisced about soccer tryouts. And Stanley Last of all.

THE FIRST TIME

Laura's mother Glow headed to the stand to tell every one about the first time Laura had a seizure.

"When Laura was born she was wonderful. She was a little colicky, but she never cried unless she was frustrated or hurt.

She fell down often, she used to scream and bite the carpet in frustration when she was learning to walk.

She'd hold her breath and hit her head in tantrums, if she didn't get what she wanted. But She was better behaved and faster when she became more mobile.

One time she grabbed a dirty nappy from the Laundry bucket, and it was covered in shit! She rubbed it into her hair right beside me.

I was so grossed out when i heard her giggle and turned around to see her playing with it like it was shampoo!

She never hit her head, She had hardly any really dangerous falls. But one day when she was about two years old, she was playing under the table and knocked her elbow on a chair leg.

She yelped and held her breath, She went red and purple and blue. She wouldn't breath, and she went rigid, fell on her side and started having a fit.

She had them more and more frequently. The doctors back then didn't have much in the way of remedy. she never seemed to have them in front of them, and going by what I was saying they figured she was deficient or febrile.

The doctor suggested Cod Liver oil, Crushed carnations, tobacco, alcohol and different diet. But they didn't work, so I turned to the church for help.

By the time they came to the house she'd gotten through most of her seizures and they suggested prayer.

It was like this for so long. I got desperate and tried baking cookies for her. Cookies with marijuana in them. It seemed to relax her a bit, but it made her eyes more sensitive and made her very tired. It was the best we had.

And we used it for a few years.

I'm ashamed to have exposed her to such things but I and she were desperate.

Her dependency on the cookies increased rapidly over the years, and by the time she was six years old she was having them all the time again. That was about the time she started school. She ended up having them at school in front of her teacher and peers, start to finish, the church freaked out and advised she stay with them.

They said they could help her, and god would save her, that she was possessed and they knew what to do!

They told me the devil was after her and that they could keep her safe.

When I said no, they turned the whole town against me! They called me a bad mother, and a whore. Saying Laura was the devils intended, and that i was harbouring a fugitive, endangering the town, by allowing an innocent child to live with so many demons.

Laura was taken from me!" she cried, "And i was forbidden to see, to visit her, or go near her... My own daughter!

Nobody wanted me at church, I was only allowed in for confession, it was the only way I could find out how she was doing.

I was given 150 Hale-Marys each time, for doubting the lord. i prayed for a miracle every day. every morning, every night, before meals, that i may one day see her again!

Finally, one confession, I discovered she had been taken by a fancy doctor. The next time i went they said he'd come back and showed them how he fixed her. But left!

And then one night she showed up on my doorstep with Stanley.

I never thought I'd see her again, or meet her rescuer! I was so happy. relieved that she was back, that i had her in my arms once more.

I know she's gone but she will always be in our hearts. And thanks to Laura I have a son inlaw, Stanley and three lovely well brought up grandchildren.

It's a terribly sad thing to out live your child! No parent should have to bury their child! It's unnatural.

The amount of guilt I feel having out lived her, knowing all the crap she went through growing up to how happy she ended up once her epilepsy was controlled to only die from another genetic disease?

It's not fair!

It's hard enough dealing with the fact your kids were fucked over for life... I don't know how Laura she managed to deal with it first hand. I wouldn't be surprised if at one point she wished she was dead, but knowing her she would have couneracted it with it's not fair that she should be made to feel thart wy and just deal with it!

Thankyou Laura for your true grit, and commitment! Your kindness, and your strength! You are a hero and someone to look up to. You're a beacon of determination inner strength and Strong will!

And I hope when any of us feel sick remember shit could be worse, and that it was for you! To take it on the chin the way you did, and tell our doubt and negativity and illness to piss off, and take a flying leap. to not let it control our heart or our life!

Thanks to your determination, you managed twenty years of a happy, healthy, safe, seizure free life. A normal life.

Something no one appreciates now days. You never took for granted and you were happy with every minute of it. Because of your determination, you've brought hope to many. And I hope your struggles, your life and your fights create a better awareness and determination to find more research on Epilepsy and other genetically related diseases."

CHILDREN AND ROCKS

Franklin, one of the poor hospital's first patients was next.

He remembered Laura from school. he remembered watching her, worried about what was happening to her and wondering why after everyone had seen how sick she was, didn't feel sorry for her.

"They were cruel to her because she was pretty, they were cruel to her because she was different. They were crueller to her about how sick she was.

I wanted to help her! But when I tried, I got shoved down the front stairs. And injured my head very badly. then I became sick, I didn't want to go to school anymore because i was afraid! Afraid that if they seen me being sick too, they'd pick on me as well!

They used to call her stupid names, pull her hair, pull down her shorts, trip her over, push her, pinch and scratch her. They'd disclude her from games, hide from her and shove her away from the play equipment.

After school, they would follow her home, teasing her! Picking up rocks and throwing them at her. If she ran they would chase her, when they caught her, they would hold her down, shove dirt in her mouth, steal her sandals and draw on her face! They would spit on her and kick her!

It was only when they heard someone coming around the corner that they would scatter. They knew what they were doing was wrong! But they did it anyway... Every day!

If there was ever evil in this town, it wasn't within Laura! When the priests decided to keep Laura at the church, and spread that stuff about her and her mother through the town, they turned everyone into demons. The town and the priests were no better than the children!

In the end my mother sent *me* to stay at the church too. I didn't fit half as much as Laura, so they figured I was less evil, and they taught me to be a productive member of the church.

Laura and I still had to sit through Sunday school with the other kids but were wre kept seperated from them, on a bench at the front of the room, we weren't allowed to play and if either of us had a seizure in sunday school, we were taken to our cells and exersized.

I wasn't in my cell the night Laura left, I was helping with the cabbage stew and the night she revisited I myself had recently had a siezure and wasn't aware of what happened.

But I was happy when I found out she was back at her mums house and that we were going to see her doctor. Laura was very kind, and silly, she had a sore leg when we seen her. She made Percy and I laugh, trying to be clever! It's scary seeing someone have a fit! Especially that night when she fell off her chair and got caught in it. It was nice to see first hand for a change though, everyone around helping out, caring! And the effects of the doctors medicines.

The medicines the doctor gave me, still work to this day. Forgetting to take them though is a dangerous business.

I heard from Laura that if you have epilepsy isolated to one part of your brain, either caused by scaring a tumour or head injury, you can have that part of your brain removed. And if you did your brain would create new pathways and connections to cope. However your chances of coping are better if it is removed at an early age. And that passed me by.

I could still do it and am considering it but I suppose I'm worried it wont turn out so good.

But I wouldn't even know if Laura hadn't told me. I guess there are some things doctors forget to tell us and some things they just don't want to.

I guess if they personally don't like your chances they wont tell you anything that will put a bee in your bonnet. That they believe its best to not give people false hope!

But I have to say, with diseases like this, you need all the hope and bright lights at the end of the tunnel youcan get. Other wise you give up, you stop striving for the summit. You just sit and mope in the darkness of a great depression. And in such cases depression can become a dangerous ally!

I hope this story I've told will make you all think twice about how you judge or decide to treat someone who is different or who's circumstances are different.

I hope this message creats a better appreciation for the need for hope.

For alternatives, and inspires doctors to think outside their textbooks! To consider anything that is non dangerous, if it has a chance of working instead of or with medication or even as a last resort should be mentioned express and explored with less taboo.

Dealing with a never ending illness takes more emotional and mental strength than anyone including educated doctors could ever understand. dealing with medically biased ignorant, naive, team yes- team no doctors who don't consider nor fathom the great deal medications effect people mentally and emotionally who would already be prone to depression and anxiety from dealing with their disease consider maybe the old fashioned more familiar way of taking the chemical road first is a bit medieval and back wards! And they will take the side effects of certain pills on ."certain patients in to a higher prioritised account to make sure they wont hurt them.

Thankyou"

WELCOME
BACK!
FIRST DAY
OF SCHOOL

FIRST DAY AT SCHOOL

The next to speak was her teacher. The only things the children were taught were about the bible, and Jesus. Every day at school was Sunday school where Laura grew up.

He took the stand and said,

"Upon Laura's first day at school, she was dressed beautifully. She sat at the front of the class. And she seemed very interested in learning the bible. More so than the others. She memorised a great many verses, and was intriguing to behold. As most children are disinterested.

She scored well. and I suppose that may have attributed to her class mates jealousy too.

I never understood how a child could be so well behaved and fixed on the bibles stories until She had a seizure at school.

She looked possessed. And maybe you could understand the children's morbid and poorly displayed curiosity towards her. By the way, thank you Franklin for telling us your experience! I had no idea she was being mistreated.

Her mother complained about her poor health and did try many therrapies including prayer. And it wasn't until i saw first hand, for myself the entire seizure, that I understood her great curiosity for the bible.

If I were her, I'd want to know too. Why me? Why am I different?

At first she sort of understood why we tried to exersize her.

But when exersism didnt work and seemed to provoke her sizures, she started to doubt and lose fait. And so did we a bit. She was a real tester. we figured she was best left locked up and alone. and I'm sorry for that!

Before she died she shared something with me. She thought she may finally understand why god put her here. As now so do I.

It wasn't just to test the church, but a great many people. As it turns out so many before her had died so suddenly in their sleep. Alone!

She was the one who would bring understanding, better medical services and a greater tolerance for those who suffer and who are different.

Just because something's different doesn't mean it's going to hurt you and so you must muzzle your instinct to weaken it.

God made all his children equal and in his image so though we are all the same we are different and though we are all different we are the same.

He makes us with our difference to test us to test our humanity, our kindness and our generosity and our nature. those who fear more are weaker and easy pray for the devil.

As it says in the bible, ‘Love thy neighbour.’

And, ‘do not judge, for as thou judge here on earth, so shall you be judged before me.’

I hope this message reaches you all on the same level.

I hope that you are all sorry, I hope you see the world through wider eyes, but not just to save you’re own skin. On the principle that you would not like to be treated the same.

I hope you fight against the injustices you whitness, and your first reaction to some one who is different, is different now to the way you treated her back then!

I pray on your conciences that you never put another living soul through what you put her through again!

On behalf of the town, I would like to thank Glow, Lauras mother for her care and hospitality, Lauras husband Stanley for all he and his friends have contributed to the health and welfare of our community. Stanley’s sister Gabby for her time and care with her patients, Laura’s children for their continued research and dedication towards the study of neurophysiology and time spent at the hospital helping out. And of course I would like to thank you Laura for all that you have done and for all you have brought to us, for living!

May the lord bless you, may he keep you. may he let you watch over those you care about. May your afterlife be a fine and happy one.

Amen!”

NOW
HIRING
So proud of you!
- Mom,
Sarah & Leo

First Job

The next to speak was Gabby. Gabby reminisced about the first day at the developing hospital, when she came in, what she'd seen, and what she'd heard.

"Laura was a clutz! When I got to glows house the first time, I was getting a briefing when I noticed Laura's bum ankle.

She was all dolled up and no where to go. Fell down the stairs running, I heard! How about that?

The next time I saw here that night, she was having a fit. Fell off her chair and got caught in it. I ran to get Stanley. It *was* a scary fit and quite lengthy. Laura was in a coma or sleep for two days, hooked up to waste bags and sodium chloride.

She couldn't remember much when she woke, but she did need to go to the toilet though. Stanley told her not to worry and to just go.

She was grossed out when she realised what he was talking about. Though she would never say it to him, because she knew he meant well. but it did make her feel depressed. she was a very proud person, she felt like her dignity went out the window. I told her she was going to do it wether she woke up or not, but she had me unhook her and help her to the bathroom anyway.

Laura didn't like to have what little independence she had available to her taken away. Even if it was something like wanting to change a few nappies when the opportunity arose becasue oh say, she had a sudden burst of energy and uninterrupted focus.

She'd get upset if you offered to do something for her after she said she'd do it. But at the same time when she did need help because she couldn't do something, she was quite often to proud or ashamed to ask, as if she feared constant judgement.

Well she never got judged by us! Her biggest enemy it seemed when it came to pride and insecurity was herself. *She* was her harshest critic.

When Laura got a bee in her bonnet it was hard to get it out! When she got upset or depressed it was hard to console her. If you looked at our point of view from her point in life, you'd be thinking whatever, you don't get it yuo'll never understand ever.

But being the beautiful person she was she would never say. If she ever did say and we tried to get her to explain it to us I don't think she could have.

She was a new woman when she was using VNS and I'm glad she stood up for herself. that she kept the bee in her bonnet to release apon the doctors! She didn't take no for an answer. At least she got some of what she wanted. She got to experience twenty years seizure free.

She was still a clutz, though that girl couldn't be trusted to remember to take her meds. Until she stopped having pettimals.

Something all of us including her doctors, should take away from this experience is, nothing is text book. Just because there is no science behind something that works yet, doesn't mean there wont be soon, should someone invent the correct monitoring device.

You specialists should yourselves hobby into finding new pathways and reasoning.

Don't judge a book by it's cover. Just because an illness looks small doesn't make it less significant, doesn't mean it's not a big deal!

Thankyou."

SOCCER TRYOUTS

Next up, the kids, the boys stood either side of their sister Sarah, and supported her as she read their letter.

"Dear mum, we don't remember you ever being sick. But we do remember all the things you did for us. And how you played with us. We remember going to preschool early for a change and we were able to choose our friends.

Our lunch boxes got fuller, and Last night we went throug all our paintings from preschool that you kept in the little black box. We remember the cubby houses you used to make with bed sheets and the stories you used to read us! The movies you took us to.

And our first soccer tryouts, when you were carrying our stuff the bench and fell over it! It was very funny and very silly. We remember you encouraging us and screaming at the b all hogs. we remember our first game which we won.

We remember you so much and so fondly, and we wish we had spent more time with you over the past years instead of the university. We know though you would never have let us take un warranted time off of our studies! And we love you for it all that much more. We miss you so much. gosh you're so stubborn! We are sorry we haven't settled down and given you the gift of grand children yet, that you had to leave us before we did!

And we hope you're proud of us and are watching over us and dad. Maybe one day when our children arrive you can watch over them too."

Sarah sobbed, "Love always Sarah, Leo and Tony. XXXX"

Stanley got up and hugged his kids and in turn gave thanks to Laura as well.

RIP

"Laura, you were my everything, my whole world. You were a beautiful, smart, funny, kind, wonderful person. And I'll never forget you.

Hopefully one day, I'll join you. But for now, I've got some kids to put through Uni, a hospital to run and soon hopefully some grandchildren to be a grandpa for.

I love you Laura!"

Stanley thanked everyone for comming and stepped down. The preacher ran a photo real of Laura with loving music.

Concluded with a prayer. Thanked everyone on behalf of Lauras family for comming, and wished them all the best.

Later at the awakening, back at the cottage... Everone stood around as Stanley planted a rose with potting soil, mixed with her ashes.

And he said to his children whilst he watered it, "Do this for me when I die? Plant a rose with potting soil and my ashes next to her and disrupt the soil between the two so we will always be together?" he asked.

"I want to be with her body and soul!" "Okay dad," they said and hugged him.

The End.

About the author

Elyse Yvonne Slater is a mother of 3, a fellow epileptic, and a passionate advocate of SUDEP and the seriousness of the daily impacts on peoples who not only suffer from epilepsy, but who are affected as carers supporting persons with epilepsy. She enjoys, writing, reading, watchig movies. Crochet, and other forms of visual art, dancing singing and acting. Epilepsy has impacted her life not only for bad, but has led her to an inward journey of personal and spiritual growth, and conscious behaviours. She is grateful to be living, loving, and to be paid for her work.

Born In and Residing in Australia, with her children, her cat, and her partner.